Professional Orchestration

ORCHESTRAL SKETCHBOOK

8.3 X 11.7, 16-STAVE PLUS PERCUSSION, UNRULED

ALEXANDER PUBLISHING
Training That Gets Results.

ALEXANDER PUBLISHING
Petersburg, Virginia

visit us at www.professionalorchestration.com

ISBN 978-0-939067-69-5

Manufactured in the United States of America
Alexander Publishing, P.O. Box 1720 Petersburg, VA 23805

PROJECT NOTES

Piccolo /
Flute

Oboe /
English Horn

Clarinet

Bassoon /
Bass Clarinet

French
Horns

Trumpets

Trombones /
Tuba

Timpani

Percussion

Violin I

Violin II

Violas

Cellos

Basses

Piccolo /
Flute

Oboe /
English Horn

Clarinet

Bassoon /
Bass Clarinet

French
Horns

Trumpets

Trombones /
Tuba

Timpani

Percussion

Violin I

Violin II

Violas

Cellos

Basses

Piccolo /
Flute

Oboe /
English Horn

Clarinet

Bassoon /
Bass Clarinet

French
Horns

Trumpets

Trombones /
Tuba

Timpani

Percussion

Violin I

Violin II

Violas

Cellos

Basses

Piccolo /
Flute

Oboe /
English Horn

Clarinet

Bassoon /
Bass Clarinet

French
Horns

Trumpets

Trombones /
Tuba

Timpani

Percussion

Violin I

Violin II

Violas

Cellos

Basses

Piccolo /
Flute

Oboe /
English Horn

Clarinet

Bassoon /
Bass Clarinet

French
Horns

Trumpets

Trombones /
Tuba

Timpani

Percussion

Violin I

Violin II

Violas

Cellos

Basses

Piccolo /
Flute

Oboe /
English Horn

Clarinet

Bassoon /
Bass Clarinet

French
Horns

Trumpets

Trombones /
Tuba

Timpani

Percussion

Violin I

Violin II

Violas

Cellos

Basses

Piccolo /
Flute

Oboe /
English Horn

Clarinet

Bassoon /
Bass Clarinet

French
Horns

Trumpets

Trombones /
Tuba

Timpani

Percussion

Violin I

Violin II

Violas

Cellos

Basses

Piccolo /
Flute

Oboe /
English Horn

Clarinet

Bassoon /
Bass Clarinet

French
Horns

Trumpets

Trombones /
Tuba

Timpani

Percussion

Violin I

Violin II

Violas

Cellos

Basses

Piccolo /
Flute

Oboe /
English Horn

Clarinet

Bassoon /
Bass Clarinet

French
Horns

Trumpets

Trombones /
Tuba

Timpani

Percussion

Violin I

Violin II

Violas

Cellos

Basses

Piccolo / Flute

Oboe / English Horn

Clarinet

Bassoon / Bass Clarinet

French Horns

Trumpets

Trombones / Tuba

Timpani

Percussion

Violin I

Violin II

Violas

Cellos

Basses

Piccolo /
Flute

Oboe /
English Horn

Clarinet

Bassoon /
Bass Clarinet

French
Horns

Trumpets

Trombones /
Tuba

Timpani

Percussion

Violin I

Violin II

Violas

Cellos

Basses

Piccolo /
Flute

Oboe /
English Horn

Clarinet

Bassoon /
Bass Clarinet

French
Horns

Trumpets

Trombones /
Tuba

Timpani

Percussion

Violin I

Violin II

Violas

Cellos

Basses

Piccolo /
Flute

Oboe /
English Horn

Clarinet

Bassoon /
Bass Clarinet

French
Horns

Trumpets

Trombones /
Tuba

Timpani

Percussion

Violin I

Violin II

Violas

Cellos

Basses

Piccolo /
Flute

Oboe /
English Horn

Clarinet

Bassoon /
Bass Clarinet

French
Horns

Trumpets

Trombones /
Tuba

Timpani

Percussion

Violin I

Violin II

Violas

Cellos

Basses

Piccolo /
Flute

Oboe /
English Horn

Clarinet

Bassoon /
Bass Clarinet

French
Horns

Trumpets

Trombones /
Tuba

Timpani

Percussion

Violin I

Violin II

Violas

Cellos

Basses

Piccolo /
Flute

Oboe /
English Horn

Clarinet

Bassoon /
Bass Clarinet

French
Horns

Trumpets

Trombones /
Tuba

Timpani

Percussion

Violin I

Violin II

Violas

Cellos

Basses

Piccolo /
Flute

Oboe /
English Horn

Clarinet

Bassoon /
Bass Clarinet

French
Horns

Trumpets

Trombones /
Tuba

Timpani

Percussion

Violin I

Violin II

Violas

Cellos

Basses

Piccolo /
Flute

Oboe /
English Horn

Clarinet

Bassoon /
Bass Clarinet

French
Horns

Trumpets

Trombones /
Tuba

Timpani

Percussion

Violin I

Violin II

Violas

Cellos

Basses

Piccolo /
Flute

Oboe /
English Horn

Clarinet

Bassoon /
Bass Clarinet

French
Horns

Trumpets

Trombones /
Tuba

Timpani

Percussion

Violin I

Violin II

Violas

Cellos

Basses

Piccolo /
Flute

Oboe /
English Horn

Clarinet

Bassoon /
Bass Clarinet

French
Horns

Trumpets

Trombones /
Tuba

Timpani

Percussion

Violin I

Violin II

Violas

Cellos

Basses

Piccolo /
Flute

Oboe /
English Horn

Clarinet

Bassoon /
Bass Clarinet

French
Horns

Trumpets

Trombones /
Tuba

Timpani

Percussion

Violin I

Violin II

Violas

Cellos

Basses

Piccolo /
Flute

Oboe /
English Horn

Clarinet

Bassoon /
Bass Clarinet

French
Horns

Trumpets

Trombones /
Tuba

Timpani

Percussion

Violin I

Violin II

Violas

Cellos

Basses

Piccolo /
Flute

Oboe /
English Horn

Clarinet

Bassoon /
Bass Clarinet

French
Horns

Trumpets

Trombones /
Tuba

Timpani

Percussion

Violin I

Violin II

Violas

Cellos

Basses

Piccolo /
Flute

Oboe /
English Horn

Clarinet

Bassoon /
Bass Clarinet

French
Horns

Trumpets

Trombones /
Tuba

Timpani

Percussion

Violin I

Violin II

Violas

Cellos

Basses

Piccolo /
Flute

Oboe /
English Horn

Clarinet

Bassoon /
Bass Clarinet

French
Horns

Trumpets

Trombones /
Tuba

Timpani

Percussion

Violin I

Violin II

Violas

Cellos

Basses

Piccolo /
Flute

Oboe /
English Horn

Clarinet

Bassoon /
Bass Clarinet

French
Horns

Trumpets

Trombones /
Tuba

Timpani

Percussion

Violin I

Violin II

Violas

Cellos

Basses

Piccolo /
Flute

Oboe /
English Horn

Clarinet

Bassoon /
Bass Clarinet

French
Horns

Trumpets

Trombones /
Tuba

Timpani

Percussion

Violin I

Violin II

Violas

Cellos

Basses

Piccolo /
Flute

Oboe /
English Horn

Clarinet

Bassoon /
Bass Clarinet

French
Horns

Trumpets

Trombones /
Tuba

Timpani

Percussion

Violin I

Violin II

Violas

Cellos

Basses

Piccolo /
Flute

Oboe /
English Horn

Clarinet

Bassoon /
Bass Clarinet

French
Horns

Trumpets

Trombones /
Tuba

Timpani

Percussion

Violin I

Violin II

Violas

Cellos

Basses

Piccolo /
Flute

Oboe /
English Horn

Clarinet

Bassoon /
Bass Clarinet

French
Horns

Trumpets

Trombones /
Tuba

Timpani

Percussion

Violin I

Violin II

Violas

Cellos

Basses

Piccolo /
Flute

Oboe /
English Horn

Clarinet

Bassoon /
Bass Clarinet

French
Horns

Trumpets

Trombones /
Tuba

Timpani

Percussion

Violin I

Violin II

Violas

Cellos

Basses

Piccolo /
Flute

Oboe /
English Horn

Clarinet

Bassoon /
Bass Clarinet

French
Horns

Trumpets

Trombones /
Tuba

Timpani

Percussion

Violin I

Violin II

Violas

Cellos

Basses

Piccolo /
Flute

Oboe /
English Horn

Clarinet

Bassoon /
Bass Clarinet

French
Horns

Trumpets

Trombones /
Tuba

Timpani

Percussion

Violin I

Violin II

Violas

Cellos

Basses

Piccolo /
Flute

Oboe /
English Horn

Clarinet

Bassoon /
Bass Clarinet

French
Horns

Trumpets

Trombones /
Tuba

Timpani

Percussion

Violin I

Violin II

Violas

Cellos

Basses

Piccolo /
Flute

Oboe /
English Horn

Clarinet

Bassoon /
Bass Clarinet

French
Horns

Trumpets

Trombones /
Tuba

Timpani

Percussion

Violin I

Violin II

Violas

Cellos

Basses

Piccolo /
Flute

Oboe /
English Horn

Clarinet

Bassoon /
Bass Clarinet

French
Horns

Trumpets

Trombones /
Tuba

Timpani

Percussion

Violin I

Violin II

Violas

Cellos

Basses

Piccolo /
Flute

Oboe /
English Horn

Clarinet

Bassoon /
Bass Clarinet

French
Horns

Trumpets

Trombones /
Tuba

Timpani

Percussion

Violin I

Violin II

Violas

Cellos

Basses

Piccolo /
Flute

Oboe /
English Horn

Clarinet

Bassoon /
Bass Clarinet

French
Horns

Trumpets

Trombones /
Tuba

Timpani

Percussion

Violin I

Violin II

Violas

Cellos

Basses

Piccolo /
Flute

Oboe /
English Horn

Clarinet

Bassoon /
Bass Clarinet

French
Horns

Trumpets

Trombones /
Tuba

Timpani

Percussion

Violin I

Violin II

Violas

Cellos

Basses

Piccolo /
Flute

Oboe /
English Horn

Clarinet

Bassoon /
Bass Clarinet

French
Horns

Trumpets

Trombones /
Tuba

Timpani

Percussion

Violin I

Violin II

Violas

Cellos

Basses

Piccolo /
Flute

Oboe /
English Horn

Clarinet

Bassoon /
Bass Clarinet

French
Horns

Trumpets

Trombones /
Tuba

Timpani

Percussion

Violin I

Violin II

Violas

Cellos

Basses

Piccolo /
Flute

Oboe /
English Horn

Clarinet

Bassoon /
Bass Clarinet

French
Horns

Trumpets

Trombones /
Tuba

Timpani

Percussion

Violin I

Violin II

Violas

Cellos

Basses

Piccolo /
Flute

Oboe /
English Horn

Clarinet

Bassoon /
Bass Clarinet

French
Horns

Trumpets

Trombones /
Tuba

Timpani

Percussion

Violin I

Violin II

Violas

Cellos

Basses

Piccolo /
Flute

Oboe /
English Horn

Clarinet

Bassoon /
Bass Clarinet

French
Horns

Trumpets

Trombones /
Tuba

Timpani

Percussion

Violin I

Violin II

Violas

Cellos

Basses

Piccolo /
Flute

Oboe /
English Horn

Clarinet

Bassoon /
Bass Clarinet

French
Horns

Trumpets

Trombones /
Tuba

Timpani

Percussion

Violin I

Violin II

Violas

Cellos

Basses

Piccolo /
Flute

Oboe /
English Horn

Clarinet

Bassoon /
Bass Clarinet

French
Horns

Trumpets

Trombones /
Tuba

Timpani

Percussion

Violin I

Violin II

Violas

Cellos

Basses

Piccolo /
Flute

Oboe /
English Horn

Clarinet

Bassoon /
Bass Clarinet

French
Horns

Trumpets

Trombones /
Tuba

Timpani

Percussion

Violin I

Violin II

Violas

Cellos

Basses

Piccolo / Flute

Oboe / English Horn

Clarinet

Bassoon / Bass Clarinet

French Horns

Trumpets

Trombones / Tuba

Timpani

Percussion

Violin I

Violin II

Violas

Cellos

Basses

Piccolo /
Flute

Oboe /
English Horn

Clarinet

Bassoon /
Bass Clarinet

French
Horns

Trumpets

Trombones /
Tuba

Timpani

Percussion

Violin I

Violin II

Violas

Cellos

Basses

Piccolo /
Flute

Oboe /
English Horn

Clarinet

Bassoon /
Bass Clarinet

French
Horns

Trumpets

Trombones /
Tuba

Timpani

Percussion

Violin I

Violin II

Violas

Cellos

Basses

Piccolo /
Flute

Oboe /
English Horn

Clarinet

Bassoon /
Bass Clarinet

French
Horns

Trumpets

Trombones /
Tuba

Timpani

Percussion

Violin I

Violin II

Violas

Cellos

Basses

Piccolo /
Flute

Oboe /
English Horn

Clarinet

Bassoon /
Bass Clarinet

French
Horns

Trumpets

Trombones /
Tuba

Timpani

Percussion

Violin I

Violin II

Violas

Cellos

Basses

Piccolo /
Flute

Oboe /
English Horn

Clarinet

Bassoon /
Bass Clarinet

French
Horns

Trumpets

Trombones /
Tuba

Timpani

Percussion

Violin I

Violin II

Violas

Cellos

Basses

Piccolo /
Flute

Oboe /
English Horn

Clarinet

Bassoon /
Bass Clarinet

French
Horns

Trumpets

Trombones /
Tuba

Timpani

Percussion

Violin I

Violin II

Violas

Cellos

Basses

Piccolo /
Flute

Oboe /
English Horn

Clarinet

Bassoon /
Bass Clarinet

French
Horns

Trumpets

Trombones /
Tuba

Timpani

Percussion

Violin I

Violin II

Violas

Cellos

Basses

Piccolo /
Flute

Oboe /
English Horn

Clarinet

Bassoon /
Bass Clarinet

French
Horns

Trumpets

Trombones /
Tuba

Timpani

Percussion

Violin I

Violin II

Violas

Cellos

Basses

Piccolo /
Flute

Oboe /
English Horn

Clarinet

Bassoon /
Bass Clarinet

French
Horns

Trumpets

Trombones /
Tuba

Timpani

Percussion

Violin I

Violin II

Violas

Cellos

Basses

Piccolo /
Flute

Oboe /
English Horn

Clarinet

Bassoon /
Bass Clarinet

French
Horns

Trumpets

Trombones /
Tuba

Timpani

Percussion

Violin I

Violin II

Violas

Cellos

Basses

Piccolo /
Flute

Oboe /
English Horn

Clarinet

Bassoon /
Bass Clarinet

French
Horns

Trumpets

Trombones /
Tuba

Timpani

Percussion

Violin I

Violin II

Violas

Cellos

Basses

Piccolo /
Flute

Oboe /
English Horn

Clarinet

Bassoon /
Bass Clarinet

French
Horns

Trumpets

Trombones /
Tuba

Timpani

Percussion

Violin I

Violin II

Violas

Cellos

Basses

Piccolo /
Flute

Oboe /
English Horn

Clarinet

Bassoon /
Bass Clarinet

French
Horns

Trumpets

Trombones /
Tuba

Timpani

Percussion

Violin I

Violin II

Violas

Cellos

Basses

Piccolo /
Flute

Oboe /
English Horn

Clarinet

Bassoon /
Bass Clarinet

French
Horns

Trumpets

Trombones /
Tuba

Timpani

Percussion

Violin I

Violin II

Violas

Cellos

Basses

Piccolo /
Flute

Oboe /
English Horn

Clarinet

Bassoon /
Bass Clarinet

French
Horns

Trumpets

Trombones /
Tuba

Timpani

Percussion

Violin I

Violin II

Violas

Cellos

Basses

Piccolo /
Flute

Oboe /
English Horn

Clarinet

Bassoon /
Bass Clarinet

French
Horns

Trumpets

Trombones /
Tuba

Timpani

Percussion

Violin I

Violin II

Violas

Cellos

Basses

Piccolo /
Flute

Oboe /
English Horn

Clarinet

Bassoon /
Bass Clarinet

French
Horns

Trumpets

Trombones /
Tuba

Timpani

Percussion

Violin I

Violin II

Violas

Cellos

Basses

Piccolo /
Flute

Oboe /
English Horn

Clarinet

Bassoon /
Bass Clarinet

French
Horns

Trumpets

Trombones /
Tuba

Timpani

Percussion

Violin I

Violin II

Violas

Cellos

Basses

Piccolo /
Flute

Oboe /
English Horn

Clarinet

Bassoon /
Bass Clarinet

French
Horns

Trumpets

Trombones /
Tuba

Timpani

Percussion

Violin I

Violin II

Violas

Cellos

Basses

Piccolo /
Flute

Oboe /
English Horn

Clarinet

Bassoon /
Bass Clarinet

French
Horns

Trumpets

Trombones /
Tuba

Timpani

Percussion

Violin I

Violin II

Violas

Cellos

Basses

Piccolo /
Flute

Oboe /
English Horn

Clarinet

Bassoon /
Bass Clarinet

French
Horns

Trumpets

Trombones /
Tuba

Timpani

Percussion

Violin I

Violin II

Violas

Cellos

Basses

Piccolo /
Flute

Oboe /
English Horn

Clarinet

Bassoon /
Bass Clarinet

French
Horns

Trumpets

Trombones /
Tuba

Timpani

Percussion

Violin I

Violin II

Violas

Cellos

Basses

Piccolo /
Flute

Oboe /
English Horn

Clarinet

Bassoon /
Bass Clarinet

French
Horns

Trumpets

Trombones /
Tuba

Timpani

Percussion

Violin I

Violin II

Violas

Cellos

Basses

Piccolo /
Flute

Oboe /
English Horn

Clarinet

Bassoon /
Bass Clarinet

French
Horns

Trumpets

Trombones /
Tuba

Timpani

Percussion

Violin I

Violin II

Violas

Cellos

Basses

Piccolo /
Flute

Oboe /
English Horn

Clarinet

Bassoon /
Bass Clarinet

French
Horns

Trumpets

Trombones /
Tuba

Timpani

Percussion

Violin I

Violin II

Violas

Cellos

Basses

Piccolo /
Flute

Oboe /
English Horn

Clarinet

Bassoon /
Bass Clarinet

French
Horns

Trumpets

Trombones /
Tuba

Timpani

Percussion

Violin I

Violin II

Violas

Cellos

Basses

Piccolo /
Flute

Oboe /
English Horn

Clarinet

Bassoon /
Bass Clarinet

French
Horns

Trumpets

Trombones /
Tuba

Timpani

Percussion

Violin I

Violin II

Violas

Cellos

Basses

Piccolo /
Flute

Oboe /
English Horn

Clarinet

Bassoon /
Bass Clarinet

French
Horns

Trumpets

Trombones /
Tuba

Timpani

Percussion

Violin I

Violin II

Violas

Cellos

Basses

Piccolo /
Flute

Oboe /
English Horn

Clarinet

Bassoon /
Bass Clarinet

French
Horns

Trumpets

Trombones /
Tuba

Timpani

Percussion

Violin I

Violin II

Violas

Cellos

Basses

Piccolo /
Flute

Oboe /
English Horn

Clarinet

Bassoon /
Bass Clarinet

French
Horns

Trumpets

Trombones /
Tuba

Timpani

Percussion

Violin I

Violin II

Violas

Cellos

Basses

Piccolo /
Flute

Oboe /
English Horn

Clarinet

Bassoon /
Bass Clarinet

French
Horns

Trumpets

Trombones /
Tuba

Timpani

Percussion

Violin I

Violin II

Violas

Cellos

Basses

Piccolo /
Flute

Oboe /
English Horn

Clarinet

Bassoon /
Bass Clarinet

French
Horns

Trumpets

Trombones /
Tuba

Timpani

Percussion

Violin I

Violin II

Violas

Cellos

Basses

SCORE: ORCH-00

Piccolo /
Flute

Oboe /
English Horn

Clarinet

Bassoon /
Bass Clarinet

French
Horns

Trumpets

Trombones /
Tuba

Timpani

Percussion

Violin I

Violin II

Violas

Cellos

Basses

Piccolo /
Flute

Oboe /
English Horn

Clarinet

Bassoon /
Bass Clarinet

French
Horns

Trumpets

Trombones /
Tuba

Timpani

Percussion

Violin I

Violin II

Violas

Cellos

Basses

Piccolo /
Flute

Oboe /
English Horn

Clarinet

Bassoon /
Bass Clarinet

French
Horns

Trumpets

Trombones /
Tuba

Timpani

Percussion

Violin I

Violin II

Violas

Cellos

Basses

Piccolo /
Flute

Oboe /
English Horn

Clarinet

Bassoon /
Bass Clarinet

French
Horns

Trumpets

Trombones /
Tuba

Timpani

Percussion

Violin I

Violin II

Violas

Cellos

Basses